MY PET

TORTOIS

CW01086151

THIS BOOK BELONGS TO:

NOTES:

MY PET
TORTOISE LOGBOOK

ALL ABOUT YOUR TORTOISE

PHOTO/DRAWING

NICKNAME:

CHARACTERTICS:

HABITAT:

COLOR /MARKING:

NOTES:

OWNER'S INFORMATION

NAME:

ADDRESS:

PHONE: EMAIL:

CRESTED GECKO'S INFORMATION

NAME: DATE OF BIRTH:

GENDER: ADOPTION PLACE:

PHONE: SPECIES:

BREED: MICROCHIP:

LICENSE#:

COLOR & MARKING:

VET INFORMATION

CLINIC: VET:

ADDRESS:

PHONE: EMAIL:

NOTES:

GROWTH CHART

DATE	WEIGHT	DATE	WEIGHT

GROWTH CHART

DATE	WEIGHT	DATE	WEIGHT

MEDICATION

MEDICATION	DATE:	NOTES:

ABOUT TORTOISE

 life span • 50 – 75 years

 Size • Around 10 –12 inch

 HUMIDITY • 50-80 %

Daily, Weekly & Monthly Activity

Daily Activity

 Feed your tortoise

 Clean and refresh water bowl

 Check correct temperatures
Check & hydrate humid
are if required

 Spot clean any waste
Remove any uneaten food

 Visually inspect tortoise

Every Other Day Activity

 Use calcium supplements

 Provide a shallow bath

Weekly Activity

 Clean glass

 Top up substrate

 Clean any decorative rocks, plants etc

 Physically inspect Tortoise

 Weigh Tortoise & record data

Monthly Activity

 Remove & replace all substrate

DAILY ACTIVITY

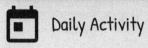 Daily Activity

WEEK OF _____ DATE _____

	SUN	MON	TUE	WED	THU	FRI	SAT
Feed Tortoise	◯	◯	◯	◯	◯	◯	◯
Clean & refresh water bowl	◯	◯	◯	◯	◯	◯	◯
Check temp / humidity	◯	◯	◯	◯	◯	◯	◯
Clean waste Remove uneaten food	◯	◯	◯	◯	◯	◯	◯
Visually inspect.	◯	◯	◯	◯	◯	◯	◯
Use calcium supplements 1 x / 2-3 day	◯	◯	◯	◯	◯	◯	◯
Provide a shallow bath 1 x / 2-3 day	◯	◯	◯	◯	◯	◯	◯

NOTES:

WEEKLY ACTIVITY

📅 DATE: _____   📅 DATE: _____

WEEKLY ACTIVITY

- ○ Clean the habitat
- ○ Top up substrate
- ○ Clean any decorative rocks, plants etc
- ○ Physically inspect
- ○ Weigh & record data
- ○ _____

HEALTH CHECKLIST

- ○ Active and alert
- ○ Eats regularly
- ○ Healthy shell
- ○ Clear, bright eyes
- ○ Healthy skin
- ○ Clear nose and vent

DIARY / NOTES:

DAILY ACTIVITY

 Daily Activity

WEEK OF ___ DATE ___

SUN MON TUE WED THU FRI SAT

 Feed Tortoise

○ ○ ○ ○ ○ ○ ○

 Clean & refresh water bowl

○ ○ ○ ○ ○ ○ ○

 Check temp / humidity

○ ○ ○ ○ ○ ○ ○

 Clean waste Remove uneaten food

○ ○ ○ ○ ○ ○ ○

 Visually inspect.

○ ○ ○ ○ ○ ○ ○

 Use calcium supplements 1 x / 2-3 day

○ ○ ○ ○ ○ ○ ○

 Provide a shallow bath 1 x / 2-3 day

○ ○ ○ ○ ○ ○ ○

NOTES:

WEEKLY ACTIVITY

☐ DATE: _____   ☐ DATE: _____

WEEKLY ACTIVITY

- ⚪ Clean the habitat
- ⚪ Top up substrate
- ⚪ Clean any decorative rocks, plants etc
- ⚪ Physically inspect
- ⚪ Weigh & record data
- ⚪ _____

HEALTH CHECKLIST

- ⚪ Active and alert
- ⚪ Eats regularly
- ⚪ Healthy shell
- ⚪ Clear, bright eyes
- ⚪ Healthy skin
- ⚪ Clear nose and vent

DIARY / NOTES:

DAILY ACTIVITY

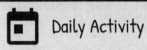 Daily Activity

WEEK OF [ ] DATE [ ]

	SUN	MON	TUE	WED	THU	FRI	SAT
Feed Tortoise	◯	◯	◯	◯	◯	◯	◯
Clean & refresh water bowl	◯	◯	◯	◯	◯	◯	◯
Check temp / humidity	◯	◯	◯	◯	◯	◯	◯
Clean waste Remove uneaten food	◯	◯	◯	◯	◯	◯	◯
Visually inspect.	◯	◯	◯	◯	◯	◯	◯
Use calcium supplements 1 x / 2-3 day	◯	◯	◯	◯	◯	◯	◯
Provide a shallow bath 1 x / 2-3 day	◯	◯	◯	◯	◯	◯	◯

NOTES:

WEEKLY ACTIVITY

📅 DATE: _____   📅 DATE: _____

WEEKLY ACTIVITY

- ○ Clean the habitat
- ○ Top up substrate
- ○ Clean any decorative rocks, plants etc
- ○ Physically inspect
- ○ Weigh & record data
- ○ _____

HEALTH CHECKLIST

- ○ Active and alert
- ○ Eats regularly
- ○ Healthy shell
- ○ Clear, bright eyes
- ○ Healthy skin
- ○ Clear nose and vent

DIARY / NOTES:

DAILY ACTIVITY

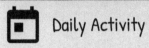 Daily Activity

WEEK OF [   ]   DATE [   ]

SUN MON TUE WED THU FRI SAT

 Feed Tortoise

○ ○ ○ ○ ○ ○ ○

 Clean & refresh water bowl

○ ○ ○ ○ ○ ○ ○

 Check temp / humidity

○ ○ ○ ○ ○ ○ ○

 Clean waste Remove uneaten food

○ ○ ○ ○ ○ ○ ○

 Visually inspect.

○ ○ ○ ○ ○ ○ ○

 Use calcium supplements 1 x / 2-3 day

○ ○ ○ ○ ○ ○ ○

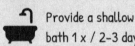 Provide a shallow bath 1 x / 2-3 day

○ ○ ○ ○ ○ ○ ○

NOTES:

WEEKLY ACTIVITY

📅 DATE: _____

📅 DATE: _____

WEEKLY ACTIVITY

- ⚪ Clean the habitat
- ⚪ Top up substrate
- ⚪ Clean any decorative rocks, plants etc
- ⚪ Physically inspect
- ⚪ Weigh & record data
- ⚪ _____

HEALTH CHECKLIST

- ⚪ Active and alert
- ⚪ Eats regularly
- ⚪ Healthy shell
- ⚪ Clear, bright eyes
- ⚪ Healthy skin
- ⚪ Clear nose and vent

DIARY / NOTES:

DAILY ACTIVITY

 Daily Activity

WEEK OF ____ DATE ____

	SUN	MON	TUE	WED	THU	FRI	SAT
Feed Tortoise	○	○	○	○	○	○	○
Clean & refresh water bowl	○	○	○	○	○	○	○
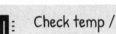 Check temp / humidity	○	○	○	○	○	○	○
Clean waste Remove uneaten food	○	○	○	○	○	○	○
Visually inspect.	○	○	○	○	○	○	○
Use calcium supplements 1 x / 2-3 day	○	○	○	○	○	○	○
Provide a shallow bath 1 x / 2-3 day	○	○	○	○	○	○	○

NOTES:

WEEKLY ACTIVITY

📅 DATE: _____ 　　📅 DATE: _____

WEEKLY ACTIVITY	HEALTH CHECKLIST
○ Clean the habitat	○ Active and alert
○ Top up substrate	○ Eats regularly
○ Clean any decorative rocks, plants etc	○ Healthy shell
○ Physically inspect	○ Clear, bright eyes
○ Weigh & record data	○ Healthy skin
	○ Clear nose and vent

DIARY / NOTES:

DAILY ACTIVITY

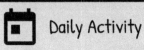 Daily Activity	WEEK OF ___ DATE ___						
	SUN	MON	TUE	WED	THU	FRI	SAT
Feed Tortoise	○	○	○	○	○	○	○
Clean & refresh water bowl	○	○	○	○	○	○	○
Check temp / humidity	○	○	○	○	○	○	○
Clean waste Remove uneaten food	○	○	○	○	○	○	○
Visually inspect.	○	○	○	○	○	○	○
Use calcium supplements 1 x / 2-3 day	○	○	○	○	○	○	○
Provide a shallow bath 1 x / 2-3 day	○	○	○	○	○	○	○

NOTES:

WEEKLY ACTIVITY

📅 DATE: 📅 DATE:

WEEKLY ACTIVITY

○ Clean the habitat

○ Top up substrate

○ Clean any decorative
rocks, plants etc

○ Physically inspect

○ Weigh & record data

HEALTH CHECKLIST

○ Active and alert

○ Eats regularly

○ Healthy shell

○ Clear, bright eyes

○ Healthy skin

○ Clear nose and vent

DIARY / NOTES:

DAILY ACTIVITY

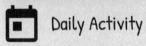 Daily Activity

WEEK OF _____ DATE _____

	SUN	MON	TUE	WED	THU	FRI	SAT
Feed Tortoise	○	○	○	○	○	○	○
Clean & refresh water bowl	○	○	○	○	○	○	○
Check temp / humidity	○	○	○	○	○	○	○
Clean waste Remove uneaten food	○	○	○	○	○	○	○
Visually inspect.	○	○	○	○	○	○	○
Use calcium supplements 1 x / 2-3 day	○	○	○	○	○	○	○
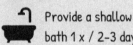 Provide a shallow bath 1 x / 2-3 day	○	○	○	○	○	○	○

NOTES:

WEEKLY ACTIVITY

📅 DATE: _____   📅 DATE: _____

WEEKLY ACTIVITY

- ○ Clean the habitat
- ○ Top up substrate
- ○ Clean any decorative rocks, plants etc
- ○ Physically inspect
- ○ Weigh & record data
- ○ _____

HEALTH CHECKLIST

- ○ Active and alert
- ○ Eats regularly
- ○ Healthy shell
- ○ Clear, bright eyes
- ○ Healthy skin
- ○ Clear nose and vent

DIARY / NOTES:

DAILY ACTIVITY

 Daily Activity

WEEK OF   DATE

SUN	MON	TUE	WED	THU	FRI	SAT

 Feed Tortoise

○ ○ ○ ○ ○ ○ ○

 Clean & refresh water bowl

○ ○ ○ ○ ○ ○ ○

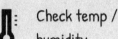 **Check temp / humidity**

○ ○ ○ ○ ○ ○ ○

 Clean waste Remove uneaten food

○ ○ ○ ○ ○ ○ ○

 Visually inspect.

○ ○ ○ ○ ○ ○ ○

 Use calcium supplements 1 x / 2-3 day

○ ○ ○ ○ ○ ○ ○

 Provide a shallow bath 1 x / 2-3 day

○ ○ ○ ○ ○ ○ ○

NOTES:

WEEKLY ACTIVITY

📅 DATE: _____   📅 DATE: _____

WEEKLY ACTIVITY

- ○ Clean the habitat
- ○ Top up substrate
- ○ Clean any decorative rocks, plants etc
- ○ Physically inspect
- ○ Weigh & record data

HEALTH CHECKLIST

- ○ Active and alert
- ○ Eats regularly
- ○ Healthy shell
- ○ Clear, bright eyes
- ○ Healthy skin
- ○ Clear nose and vent

DIARY / NOTES:

DAILY ACTIVITY

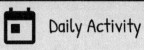 Daily Activity	WEEK OF DATE
	SUN MON TUE WED THU FRI SAT

Feed Tortoise	○ ○ ○ ○ ○ ○ ○

Clean & refresh water bowl	○ ○ ○ ○ ○ ○ ○

Check temp / humidity	○ ○ ○ ○ ○ ○ ○

Clean waste Remove uneaten food	○ ○ ○ ○ ○ ○ ○

Visually inspect.	○ ○ ○ ○ ○ ○ ○

Use calcium supplements 1 x / 2-3 day	○ ○ ○ ○ ○ ○ ○

Provide a shallow bath 1 x / 2-3 day	○ ○ ○ ○ ○ ○ ○

NOTES:

WEEKLY ACTIVITY

📅 DATE: _____

📅 DATE: _____

WEEKLY ACTIVITY

- ○ Clean the habitat
- ○ Top up substrate
- ○ Clean any decorative rocks, plants etc
- ○ Physically inspect
- ○ Weigh & record data
  _____

HEALTH CHECKLIST

- ○ Active and alert
- ○ Eats regularly
- ○ Healthy shell
- ○ Clear, bright eyes
- ○ Healthy skin
- ○ Clear nose and vent

DIARY / NOTES:

DAILY ACTIVITY

 Daily Activity

WEEK OF _____ DATE _____

	SUN	MON	TUE	WED	THU	FRI	SAT
Feed Tortoise	○	○	○	○	○	○	○
Clean & refresh water bowl	○	○	○	○	○	○	○
Check temp / humidity	○	○	○	○	○	○	○
Clean waste Remove uneaten food	○	○	○	○	○	○	○
Visually inspect.	○	○	○	○	○	○	○
Use calcium supplements 1 x / 2-3 day	○	○	○	○	○	○	○
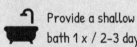 Provide a shallow bath 1 x / 2-3 day	○	○	○	○	○	○	○

NOTES:

WEEKLY ACTIVITY

📅 DATE: _____

📅 DATE: _____

WEEKLY ACTIVITY

- ⚪ Clean the habitat
- ⚪ Top up substrate
- ⚪ Clean any decorative rocks, plants etc
- ⚪ Physically inspect
- ⚪ Weigh & record data

HEALTH CHECKLIST

- ⚪ Active and alert
- ⚪ Eats regularly
- ⚪ Healthy shell
- ⚪ Clear, bright eyes
- ⚪ Healthy skin
- ⚪ Clear nose and vent

DIARY / NOTES:

DAILY ACTIVITY

 Daily Activity

WEEK OF [____] DATE [____]

	SUN	MON	TUE	WED	THU	FRI	SAT

 Feed Tortoise ○ ○ ○ ○ ○ ○ ○

Clean & refresh water bowl ○ ○ ○ ○ ○ ○ ○

 Check temp / humidity ○ ○ ○ ○ ○ ○ ○

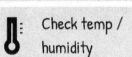 Clean waste
Remove uneaten food ○ ○ ○ ○ ○ ○ ○

 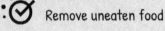 Visually inspect. ○ ○ ○ ○ ○ ○ ○

 20 Ca Use calcium supplements 1 x / 2-3 day ○ ○ ○ ○ ○ ○ ○

 Provide a shallow bath 1 x / 2-3 day ○ ○ ○ ○ ○ ○ ○

NOTES:

WEEKLY ACTIVITY

📅 DATE: _____

📅 DATE: _____

WEEKLY ACTIVITY

- ○ Clean the habitat
- ○ Top up substrate
- ○ Clean any decorative rocks, plants etc
- ○ Physically inspect
- ○ Weigh & record data

HEALTH CHECKLIST

- ○ Active and alert
- ○ Eats regularly
- ○ Healthy shell
- ○ Clear, bright eyes
- ○ Healthy skin
- ○ Clear nose and vent

DIARY / NOTES:

DAILY ACTIVITY

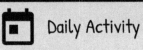 Daily Activity

WEEK OF _____ DATE _____

SUN MON TUE WED THU FRI SAT

 Feed Tortoise
○ ○ ○ ○ ○ ○ ○

 Clean & refresh water bowl
○ ○ ○ ○ ○ ○ ○

 Check temp / humidity
○ ○ ○ ○ ○ ○ ○

 Clean waste
Remove uneaten food
○ ○ ○ ○ ○ ○ ○

 Visually inspect.
○ ○ ○ ○ ○ ○ ○

 Use calcium supplements 1 x / 2-3 day
○ ○ ○ ○ ○ ○ ○

 Provide a shallow bath 1 x / 2-3 day
○ ○ ○ ○ ○ ○ ○

NOTES:

WEEKLY ACTIVITY

📅 DATE: _____   📅 DATE: _____

WEEKLY ACTIVITY

- ○ Clean the habitat
- ○ Top up substrate
- ○ Clean any decorative rocks, plants etc
- ○ Physically inspect
- ○ Weigh & record data
  _____

HEALTH CHECKLIST

- ○ Active and alert
- ○ Eats regularly
- ○ Healthy shell
- ○ Clear, bright eyes
- ○ Healthy skin
- ○ Clear nose and vent

DIARY / NOTES:

DAILY ACTIVITY

 Daily Activity

WEEK OF _____ DATE _____

	SUN	MON	TUE	WED	THU	FRI	SAT
Feed Tortoise	○	○	○	○	○	○	○
Clean & refresh water bowl	○	○	○	○	○	○	○
Check temp / humidity	○	○	○	○	○	○	○
Clean waste Remove uneaten food	○	○	○	○	○	○	○
Visually inspect.	○	○	○	○	○	○	○
Use calcium supplements 1 x / 2-3 day	○	○	○	○	○	○	○
Provide a shallow bath 1 x / 2-3 day	○	○	○	○	○	○	○

NOTES:

WEEKLY ACTIVITY

📅 DATE: _____   📅 DATE: _____

WEEKLY ACTIVITY

- ○ Clean the habitat
- ○ Top up substrate
- ○ Clean any decorative rocks, plants etc
- ○ Physically inspect
- ○ Weigh & record data
- ○ _____

HEALTH CHECKLIST

- ○ Active and alert
- ○ Eats regularly
- ○ Healthy shell
- ○ Clear, bright eyes
- ○ Healthy skin
- ○ Clear nose and vent

DIARY / NOTES:

DAILY ACTIVITY

 Daily Activity

WEEK OF [ ] DATE [ ]

	SUN	MON	TUE	WED	THU	FRI	SAT
Feed Tortoise	○	○	○	○	○	○	○
Clean & refresh water bowl	○	○	○	○	○	○	○
Check temp / humidity	○	○	○	○	○	○	○
Clean waste Remove uneaten food	○	○	○	○	○	○	○
Visually inspect.	○	○	○	○	○	○	○
Use calcium supplements 1 x / 2-3 day	○	○	○	○	○	○	○
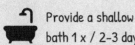 Provide a shallow bath 1 x / 2-3 day	○	○	○	○	○	○	○

NOTES:

WEEKLY ACTIVITY

📅 DATE: [_____]   📅 DATE: [_____]

WEEKLY ACTIVITY

- ○ Clean the habitat
- ○ Top up substrate
- ○ Clean any decorative rocks, plants etc
- ○ Physically inspect
- ○ Weigh & record data
  [_____]

HEALTH CHECKLIST

- ○ Active and alert
- ○ Eats regularly
- ○ Healthy shell
- ○ Clear, bright eyes
- ○ Healthy skin
- ○ Clear nose and vent

DIARY / NOTES:

DAILY ACTIVITY

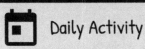 Daily Activity

WEEK OF _____ DATE _____

	SUN	MON	TUE	WED	THU	FRI	SAT

 Feed Tortoise ⚪ ⚪ ⚪ ⚪ ⚪ ⚪ ⚪

 Clean & refresh water bowl ⚪ ⚪ ⚪ ⚪ ⚪ ⚪ ⚪

 Check temp / humidity ⚪ ⚪ ⚪ ⚪ ⚪ ⚪ ⚪

 Clean waste Remove uneaten food ⚪ ⚪ ⚪ ⚪ ⚪ ⚪ ⚪

 Visually inspect. ⚪ ⚪ ⚪ ⚪ ⚪ ⚪ ⚪

 Use calcium supplements 1 x / 2-3 day ⚪ ⚪ ⚪ ⚪ ⚪ ⚪ ⚪

 Provide a shallow bath 1 x / 2-3 day ⚪ ⚪ ⚪ ⚪ ⚪ ⚪ ⚪

NOTES:

WEEKLY ACTIVITY

📅 DATE: _____   📅 DATE: _____

WEEKLY ACTIVITY

- ⚪ Clean the habitat
- ⚪ Top up substrate
- ⚪ Clean any decorative rocks, plants etc
- ⚪ Physically inspect
- ⚪ Weigh & record data

HEALTH CHECKLIST

- ⚪ Active and alert
- ⚪ Eats regularly
- ⚪ Healthy shell
- ⚪ Clear, bright eyes
- ⚪ Healthy skin
- ⚪ Clear nose and vent

DIARY / NOTES:

DAILY ACTIVITY

 Daily Activity

WEEK OF _____ **DATE** _____

	SUN	MON	TUE	WED	THU	FRI	SAT

 Feed Tortoise ⬤ ⬤ ⬤ ⬤ ⬤ ⬤ ⬤

 Clean & refresh water bowl ⬤ ⬤ ⬤ ⬤ ⬤ ⬤ ⬤

 Check temp / humidity ⬤ ⬤ ⬤ ⬤ ⬤ ⬤ ⬤

 Clean waste Remove uneaten food ⬤ ⬤ ⬤ ⬤ ⬤ ⬤ ⬤

 Visually inspect. ⬤ ⬤ ⬤ ⬤ ⬤ ⬤ ⬤

 Use calcium supplements 1 x / 2-3 day ⬤ ⬤ ⬤ ⬤ ⬤ ⬤ ⬤

Provide a shallow bath 1 x / 2-3 day ⬤ ⬤ ⬤ ⬤ ⬤ ⬤ ⬤

NOTES:

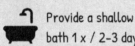

WEEKLY ACTIVITY

📅 DATE: _____   📅 DATE: _____

WEEKLY ACTIVITY

- ⚪ Clean the habitat
- ⚪ Top up substrate
- ⚪ Clean any decorative rocks, plants etc
- ⚪ Physically inspect
- ⚪ Weigh & record data

HEALTH CHECKLIST

- ⚪ Active and alert
- ⚪ Eats regularly
- ⚪ Healthy shell
- ⚪ Clear, bright eyes
- ⚪ Healthy skin
- ⚪ Clear nose and vent

DIARY / NOTES:

DAILY ACTIVITY

 Daily Activity

WEEK OF ☐ DATE ☐

	SUN	MON	TUE	WED	THU	FRI	SAT
Feed Tortoise	○	○	○	○	○	○	○
Clean & refresh water bowl	○	○	○	○	○	○	○
Check temp / humidity	○	○	○	○	○	○	○
Clean waste Remove uneaten food	○	○	○	○	○	○	○
Visually inspect.	○	○	○	○	○	○	○
Use calcium supplements 1 x / 2-3 day	○	○	○	○	○	○	○
Provide a shallow bath 1 x / 2-3 day	○	○	○	○	○	○	○

NOTES:

WEEKLY ACTIVITY

 DATE: _____   📅 DATE: _____

WEEKLY ACTIVITY	HEALTH CHECKLIST
○ Clean the habitat	○ Active and alert
○ Top up substrate	○ Eats regularly
○ Clean any decorative rocks, plants etc	○ Healthy shell
○ Physically inspect	○ Clear, bright eyes
○ Weigh & record data	○ Healthy skin
	○ Clear nose and vent

DIARY / NOTES:

DAILY ACTIVITY

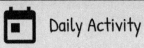 Daily Activity

WEEK OF _____ DATE _____

	SUN	MON	TUE	WED	THU	FRI	SAT

 Feed Tortoise ○ ○ ○ ○ ○ ○ ○

 Clean & refresh water bowl ○ ○ ○ ○ ○ ○ ○

 Check temp / humidity ○ ○ ○ ○ ○ ○ ○

 Clean waste Remove uneaten food ○ ○ ○ ○ ○ ○ ○

 Visually inspect. ○ ○ ○ ○ ○ ○ ○

 Use calcium supplements 1 x / 2-3 day ○ ○ ○ ○ ○ ○ ○

 Provide a shallow bath 1 x / 2-3 day ○ ○ ○ ○ ○ ○ ○

NOTES:

WEEKLY ACTIVITY

📅 DATE: _____   📅 DATE: _____

WEEKLY ACTIVITY

- ⚪ Clean the habitat
- ⚪ Top up substrate
- ⚪ Clean any decorative rocks, plants etc
- ⚪ Physically inspect
- ⚪ Weigh & record data

HEALTH CHECKLIST

- ⚪ Active and alert
- ⚪ Eats regularly
- ⚪ Healthy shell
- ⚪ Clear, bright eyes
- ⚪ Healthy skin
- ⚪ Clear nose and vent

DIARY / NOTES:

DAILY ACTIVITY

 Daily Activity

WEEK OF _____ DATE _____

	SUN	MON	TUE	WED	THU	FRI	SAT
Feed Tortoise	○	○	○	○	○	○	○
Clean & refresh water bowl	○	○	○	○	○	○	○
Check temp / humidity	○	○	○	○	○	○	○
Clean waste Remove uneaten food	○	○	○	○	○	○	○
Visually inspect.	○	○	○	○	○	○	○
Use calcium supplements 1 x / 2-3 day	○	○	○	○	○	○	○
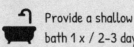 Provide a shallow bath 1 x / 2-3 day	○	○	○	○	○	○	○

NOTES:

WEEKLY ACTIVITY

📅 DATE: _____   📅 DATE: _____

WEEKLY ACTIVITY

- ⚪ Clean the habitat
- ⚪ Top up substrate
- ⚪ Clean any decorative rocks, plants etc
- ⚪ Physically inspect
- ⚪ Weigh & record data
- ⚪ _____

HEALTH CHECKLIST

- ⚪ Active and alert
- ⚪ Eats regularly
- ⚪ Healthy shell
- ⚪ Clear, bright eyes
- ⚪ Healthy skin
- ⚪ Clear nose and vent

DIARY / NOTES:

DAILY ACTIVITY

 Daily Activity

WEEK OF [ ] DATE [ ]

	SUN	MON	TUE	WED	THU	FRI	SAT
Feed Tortoise	○	○	○	○	○	○	○
Clean & refresh water bowl	○	○	○	○	○	○	○
Check temp / humidity	○	○	○	○	○	○	○
Clean waste Remove uneaten food	○	○	○	○	○	○	○
Visually inspect.	○	○	○	○	○	○	○
Use calcium supplements 1 x / 2-3 day	○	○	○	○	○	○	○
Provide a shallow bath 1 x / 2-3 day	○	○	○	○	○	○	○

NOTES:

WEEKLY ACTIVITY

📅 DATE: _____   📅 DATE: _____

WEEKLY ACTIVITY

- ○ Clean the habitat
- ○ Top up substrate
- ○ Clean any decorative rocks, plants etc
- ○ Physically inspect
- ○ Weigh & record data
  - _____

HEALTH CHECKLIST

- ○ Active and alert
- ○ Eats regularly
- ○ Healthy shell
- ○ Clear, bright eyes
- ○ Healthy skin
- ○ Clear nose and vent

DIARY / NOTES:

DAILY ACTIVITY

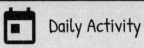 Daily Activity

WEEK OF ____ DATE _____

	SUN	MON	TUE	WED	THU	FRI	SAT

 Feed Tortoise
○ ○ ○ ○ ○ ○ ○

 Clean & refresh water bowl
○ ○ ○ ○ ○ ○ ○

 Check temp / humidity
○ ○ ○ ○ ○ ○ ○

 Clean waste Remove uneaten food
○ ○ ○ ○ ○ ○ ○

 Visually inspect.
○ ○ ○ ○ ○ ○ ○

 Use calcium supplements 1 x / 2-3 day
○ ○ ○ ○ ○ ○ ○

 Provide a shallow bath 1 x / 2-3 day
○ ○ ○ ○ ○ ○ ○

NOTES:

WEEKLY ACTIVITY

📅 DATE: _____   📅 DATE: _____

WEEKLY ACTIVITY

- ⚪ Clean the habitat
- ⚪ Top up substrate
- ⚪ Clean any decorative rocks, plants etc
- ⚪ Physically inspect
- ⚪ Weigh & record data

HEALTH CHECKLIST

- ⚪ Active and alert
- ⚪ Eats regularly
- ⚪ Healthy shell
- ⚪ Clear, bright eyes
- ⚪ Healthy skin
- ⚪ Clear nose and vent

DIARY / NOTES:

DAILY ACTIVITY

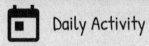 Daily Activity

WEEK OF ____ DATE ____

	SUN	MON	TUE	WED	THU	FRI	SAT
Feed Tortoise	○	○	○	○	○	○	○
Clean & refresh water bowl	○	○	○	○	○	○	○
Check temp / humidity	○	○	○	○	○	○	○
Clean waste Remove uneaten food	○	○	○	○	○	○	○
Visually inspect.	○	○	○	○	○	○	○
Use calcium supplements 1 x / 2-3 day	○	○	○	○	○	○	○
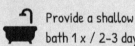 Provide a shallow bath 1 x / 2-3 day	○	○	○	○	○	○	○

NOTES:

WEEKLY ACTIVITY

📅 DATE: _____   📅 DATE: _____

WEEKLY ACTIVITY

- ⚪ Clean the habitat
- ⚪ Top up substrate
- ⚪ Clean any decorative rocks, plants etc
- ⚪ Physically inspect
- ⚪ Weigh & record data
  - _____

HEALTH CHECKLIST

- ⚪ Active and alert
- ⚪ Eats regularly
- ⚪ Healthy shell
- ⚪ Clear, bright eyes
- ⚪ Healthy skin
- ⚪ Clear nose and vent

DIARY / NOTES:

DAILY ACTIVITY

 Daily Activity

WEEK OF ____ DATE ____

	SUN	MON	TUE	WED	THU	FRI	SAT
Feed Tortoise	○	○	○	○	○	○	○
Clean & refresh water bowl	○	○	○	○	○	○	○
Check temp / humidity	○	○	○	○	○	○	○
Clean waste Remove uneaten food	○	○	○	○	○	○	○
Visually inspect.	○	○	○	○	○	○	○
Use calcium supplements 1 x / 2-3 day	○	○	○	○	○	○	○
Provide a shallow bath 1 x / 2-3 day	○	○	○	○	○	○	○

NOTES:

WEEKLY ACTIVITY

 DATE: _____

📅 DATE: _____

WEEKLY ACTIVITY

○ Clean the habitat

○ Top up substrate

○ Clean any decorative rocks, plants etc

○ Physically inspect

○ Weigh & record data

HEALTH CHECKLIST

○ Active and alert

○ Eats regularly

○ Healthy shell

○ Clear, bright eyes

○ Healthy skin

○ Clear nose and vent

DIARY / NOTES:

DAILY ACTIVITY

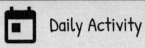 Daily Activity

WEEK OF _____ DATE _____

	SUN	MON	TUE	WED	THU	FRI	SAT
Feed Tortoise	○	○	○	○	○	○	○
Clean & refresh water bowl	○	○	○	○	○	○	○
Check temp / humidity	○	○	○	○	○	○	○
Clean waste Remove uneaten food	○	○	○	○	○	○	○
Visually inspect.	○	○	○	○	○	○	○
Use calcium supplements 1 x / 2-3 day	○	○	○	○	○	○	○
Provide a shallow bath 1 x / 2-3 day	○	○	○	○	○	○	○

NOTES:

WEEKLY ACTIVITY

📅 DATE: _____   📅 DATE: _____

WEEKLY ACTIVITY

- ⚪ Clean the habitat
- ⚪ Top up substrate
- ⚪ Clean any decorative rocks, plants etc
- ⚪ Physically inspect
- ⚪ Weigh & record data

_____

HEALTH CHECKLIST

- ⚪ Active and alert
- ⚪ Eats regularly
- ⚪ Healthy shell
- ⚪ Clear, bright eyes
- ⚪ Healthy skin
- ⚪ Clear nose and vent

DIARY / NOTES:

DAILY ACTIVITY

 Daily Activity

WEEK OF ____ DATE ____

	SUN	MON	TUE	WED	THU	FRI	SAT
Feed Tortoise	○	○	○	○	○	○	○
Clean & refresh water bowl	○	○	○	○	○	○	○
Check temp / humidity	○	○	○	○	○	○	○
Clean waste Remove uneaten food	○	○	○	○	○	○	○
Visually inspect.	○	○	○	○	○	○	○
Use calcium supplements 1 x / 2-3 day	○	○	○	○	○	○	○
Provide a shallow bath 1 x / 2-3 day	○	○	○	○	○	○	○

NOTES:

WEEKLY ACTIVITY

📅 DATE: _____   📅 DATE: _____

WEEKLY ACTIVITY

○ Clean the habitat

○ Top up substrate

○ Clean any decorative rocks, plants etc

○ Physically inspect

○ Weigh & record data

_____

HEALTH CHECKLIST

○ Active and alert

○ Eats regularly

○ Healthy shell

○ Clear, bright eyes

○ Healthy skin

○ Clear nose and vent

DIARY / NOTES:

DAILY ACTIVITY

 Daily Activity

WEEK OF [ ] DATE [ ]

	SUN	MON	TUE	WED	THU	FRI	SAT
Feed Tortoise	○	○	○	○	○	○	○
Clean & refresh water bowl	○	○	○	○	○	○	○
Check temp / humidity	○	○	○	○	○	○	○
Clean waste Remove uneaten food	○	○	○	○	○	○	○
Visually inspect.	○	○	○	○	○	○	○
Use calcium supplements 1 x / 2-3 day	○	○	○	○	○	○	○
Provide a shallow bath 1 x / 2-3 day	○	○	○	○	○	○	○

NOTES:

WEEKLY ACTIVITY

📅 DATE: _____   📅 DATE: _____

WEEKLY ACTIVITY

- ○ Clean the habitat
- ○ Top up substrate
- ○ Clean any decorative rocks, plants etc
- ○ Physically inspect
- ○ Weigh & record data
- ○ _____

HEALTH CHECKLIST

- ○ Active and alert
- ○ Eats regularly
- ○ Healthy shell
- ○ Clear, bright eyes
- ○ Healthy skin
- ○ Clear nose and vent

DIARY / NOTES:

DAILY ACTIVITY

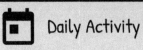 Daily Activity

WEEK OF ____ DATE ____

	SUN	MON	TUE	WED	THU	FRI	SAT
Feed Tortoise	○	○	○	○	○	○	○
Clean & refresh water bowl	○	○	○	○	○	○	○
Check temp / humidity	○	○	○	○	○	○	○
Clean waste Remove uneaten food	○	○	○	○	○	○	○
Visually inspect.	○	○	○	○	○	○	○
Use calcium supplements 1 x / 2-3 day	○	○	○	○	○	○	○
Provide a shallow bath 1 x / 2-3 day	○	○	○	○	○	○	○

NOTES:

WEEKLY ACTIVITY

📅 DATE: _____   📅 DATE: _____

WEEKLY ACTIVITY	HEALTH CHECKLIST
○ Clean the habitat	○ Active and alert
○ Top up substrate	○ Eats regularly
○ Clean any decorative rocks, plants etc	○ Healthy shell
○ Physically inspect	○ Clear, bright eyes
○ Weigh & record data _____	○ Healthy skin
	○ Clear nose and vent

DIARY / NOTES:

DAILY ACTIVITY

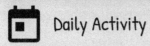 Daily Activity

	SUN	MON	TUE	WED	THU	FRI	SAT

WEEK OF [   ] DATE [   ]

Activity	SUN	MON	TUE	WED	THU	FRI	SAT
Feed Tortoise	○	○	○	○	○	○	○
Clean & refresh water bowl	○	○	○	○	○	○	○
Check temp / humidity	○	○	○	○	○	○	○
Clean waste Remove uneaten food	○	○	○	○	○	○	○
Visually inspect.	○	○	○	○	○	○	○
Use calcium supplements 1 x / 2-3 day	○	○	○	○	○	○	○
Provide a shallow bath 1 x / 2-3 day	○	○	○	○	○	○	○

NOTES:

WEEKLY ACTIVITY

📅 DATE: _____   📅 DATE: _____

WEEKLY ACTIVITY

- ○ Clean the habitat
- ○ Top up substrate
- ○ Clean any decorative rocks, plants etc
- ○ Physically inspect
- ○ Weigh & record data

HEALTH CHECKLIST

- ○ Active and alert
- ○ Eats regularly
- ○ Healthy shell
- ○ Clear, bright eyes
- ○ Healthy skin
- ○ Clear nose and vent

DIARY / NOTES:

DAILY ACTIVITY

 Daily Activity

WEEK OF [   ] DATE [   ]

	SUN	MON	TUE	WED	THU	FRI	SAT
Feed Tortoise	○	○	○	○	○	○	○
Clean & refresh water bowl	○	○	○	○	○	○	○
Check temp / humidity	○	○	○	○	○	○	○
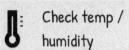 Clean waste Remove uneaten food	○	○	○	○	○	○	○
Visually inspect.	○	○	○	○	○	○	○
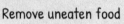 Use calcium supplements 1 x / 2-3 day	○	○	○	○	○	○	○
Provide a shallow bath 1 x / 2-3 day	○	○	○	○	○	○	○

NOTES:

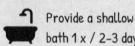

WEEKLY ACTIVITY

📅 DATE: _____   📅 DATE: _____

WEEKLY ACTIVITY

- ○ Clean the habitat
- ○ Top up substrate
- ○ Clean any decorative rocks, plants etc
- ○ Physically inspect
- ○ Weigh & record data
  - [_____]

HEALTH CHECKLIST

- ○ Active and alert
- ○ Eats regularly
- ○ Healthy shell
- ○ Clear, bright eyes
- ○ Healthy skin
- ○ Clear nose and vent

DIARY / NOTES:

DAILY ACTIVITY

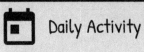 Daily Activity	WEEK OF ___ DATE ___						
	SUN	MON	TUE	WED	THU	FRI	SAT
Feed Tortoise	○	○	○	○	○	○	○
Clean & refresh water bowl	○	○	○	○	○	○	○
Check temp / humidity	○	○	○	○	○	○	○
Clean waste Remove uneaten food	○	○	○	○	○	○	○
Visually inspect.	○	○	○	○	○	○	○
Use calcium supplements 1 x / 2-3 day	○	○	○	○	○	○	○
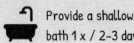 Provide a shallow bath 1 x / 2-3 day	○	○	○	○	○	○	○

NOTES:

WEEKLY ACTIVITY

📅 DATE: _____   📅 DATE: _____

WEEKLY ACTIVITY

- ☐ Clean the habitat
- ☐ Top up substrate
- ☐ Clean any decorative rocks, plants etc
- ☐ Physically inspect
- ☐ Weigh & record data
  ☐ _____

HEALTH CHECKLIST

- ☐ Active and alert
- ☐ Eats regularly
- ☐ Healthy shell
- ☐ Clear, bright eyes
- ☐ Healthy skin
- ☐ Clear nose and vent

DIARY / NOTES:

DAILY ACTIVITY

 Daily Activity

WEEK OF ____ DATE ____

SUN MON TUE WED THU FRI SAT

 Feed Tortoise

○ ○ ○ ○ ○ ○ ○

 Clean & refresh water bowl

○ ○ ○ ○ ○ ○ ○

 Check temp / humidity

○ ○ ○ ○ ○ ○ ○

 Clean waste Remove uneaten food

○ ○ ○ ○ ○ ○ ○

 Visually inspect.

○ ○ ○ ○ ○ ○ ○

 Use calcium supplements 1 x / 2-3 day

○ ○ ○ ○ ○ ○ ○

 Provide a shallow bath 1 x / 2-3 day

○ ○ ○ ○ ○ ○ ○

NOTES:

WEEKLY ACTIVITY

📅 DATE: _____   📅 DATE: _____

WEEKLY ACTIVITY

- ◯ Clean the habitat
- ◯ Top up substrate
- ◯ Clean any decorative rocks, plants etc
- ◯ Physically inspect
- ◯ Weigh & record data
- ◯ _____

HEALTH CHECKLIST

- ◯ Active and alert
- ◯ Eats regularly
- ◯ Healthy shell
- ◯ Clear, bright eyes
- ◯ Healthy skin
- ◯ Clear nose and vent

DIARY / NOTES:

DAILY ACTIVITY

 Daily Activity

WEEK OF _____ DATE _____

	SUN	MON	TUE	WED	THU	FRI	SAT
Feed Tortoise	○	○	○	○	○	○	○
Clean & refresh water bowl	○	○	○	○	○	○	○
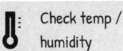 Check temp / humidity	○	○	○	○	○	○	○
Clean waste Remove uneaten food	○	○	○	○	○	○	○
Visually inspect.	○	○	○	○	○	○	○
Use calcium supplements 1 x / 2-3 day	○	○	○	○	○	○	○
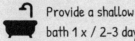 Provide a shallow bath 1 x / 2-3 day	○	○	○	○	○	○	○

NOTES:

WEEKLY ACTIVITY

📅 DATE: _____   📅 DATE: _____

WEEKLY ACTIVITY

- ○ Clean the habitat
- ○ Top up substrate
- ○ Clean any decorative rocks, plants etc
- ○ Physically inspect
- ○ Weigh & record data

HEALTH CHECKLIST

- ○ Active and alert
- ○ Eats regularly
- ○ Healthy shell
- ○ Clear, bright eyes
- ○ Healthy skin
- ○ Clear nose and vent

DIARY / NOTES:

DAILY ACTIVITY

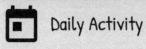 Daily Activity	WEEK OF _____ DATE _____						
	SUN	MON	TUE	WED	THU	FRI	SAT
Feed Tortoise	○	○	○	○	○	○	○
Clean & refresh water bowl	○	○	○	○	○	○	○
Check temp / humidity	○	○	○	○	○	○	○
Clean waste Remove uneaten food	○	○	○	○	○	○	○
Visually inspect.	○	○	○	○	○	○	○
Use calcium supplements 1 x / 2-3 day	○	○	○	○	○	○	○
Provide a shallow bath 1 x / 2-3 day	○	○	○	○	○	○	○

NOTES:

WEEKLY ACTIVITY

📅 DATE: _____   📅 DATE: _____

WEEKLY ACTIVITY

- ○ Clean the habitat
- ○ Top up substrate
- ○ Clean any decorative rocks, plants etc
- ○ Physically inspect
- ○ Weigh & record data
  _____

HEALTH CHECKLIST

- ○ Active and alert
- ○ Eats regularly
- ○ Healthy shell
- ○ Clear, bright eyes
- ○ Healthy skin
- ○ Clear nose and vent

DIARY / NOTES:

DAILY ACTIVITY

	Daily Activity	WEEK OF	DATE					
		SUN	MON	TUE	WED	THU	FRI	SAT
	Feed Tortoise	○	○	○	○	○	○	○
	Clean & refresh water bowl	○	○	○	○	○	○	○
	Check temp / humidity	○	○	○	○	○	○	○
	Clean waste Remove uneaten food	○	○	○	○	○	○	○
	Visually inspect.	○	○	○	○	○	○	○
	Use calcium supplements 1 x / 2-3 day	○	○	○	○	○	○	○
	Provide a shallow bath 1 x / 2-3 day	○	○	○	○	○	○	○

NOTES:

WEEKLY ACTIVITY

📅 DATE: _____   📅 DATE: _____

WEEKLY ACTIVITY

- ○ Clean the habitat
- ○ Top up substrate
- ○ Clean any decorative rocks, plants etc
- ○ Physically inspect
- ○ Weigh & record data
- ○ _____

HEALTH CHECKLIST

- ○ Active and alert
- ○ Eats regularly
- ○ Healthy shell
- ○ Clear, bright eyes
- ○ Healthy skin
- ○ Clear nose and vent

DIARY / NOTES:

DAILY ACTIVITY

 Daily Activity

	WEEK OF	DATE				
SUN	MON	TUE	WED	THU	FRI	SAT

 Feed Tortoise

 Clean & refresh water bowl

 Check temp / humidity

 Clean waste
Remove uneaten food

 Visually inspect.

 Use calcium supplements 1 x / 2-3 day

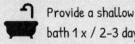 Provide a shallow bath 1 x / 2-3 day

NOTES:

WEEKLY ACTIVITY

📅 DATE: _____   📅 DATE: _____

WEEKLY ACTIVITY

- ◯ Clean the habitat
- ◯ Top up substrate
- ◯ Clean any decorative rocks, plants etc
- ◯ Physically inspect
- ◯ Weigh & record data
- ◯ _____

HEALTH CHECKLIST

- ◯ Active and alert
- ◯ Eats regularly
- ◯ Healthy shell
- ◯ Clear, bright eyes
- ◯ Healthy skin
- ◯ Clear nose and vent

DIARY / NOTES:

DAILY ACTIVITY

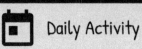 Daily Activity

WEEK OF _____ DATE _____

SUN MON TUE WED THU FRI SAT

 Feed Tortoise ○ ○ ○ ○ ○ ○ ○

 Clean & refresh water bowl ○ ○ ○ ○ ○ ○ ○

 Check temp / humidity ○ ○ ○ ○ ○ ○ ○

 Clean waste Remove uneaten food ○ ○ ○ ○ ○ ○ ○

 Visually inspect. ○ ○ ○ ○ ○ ○ ○

 Use calcium supplements 1 x / 2-3 day ○ ○ ○ ○ ○ ○ ○

 Provide a shallow bath 1 x / 2-3 day ○ ○ ○ ○ ○ ○ ○

NOTES:

WEEKLY ACTIVITY

📅 DATE:

📅 DATE:

WEEKLY ACTIVITY

○ Clean the habitat

○ Top up substrate

○ Clean any decorative rocks, plants etc

○ Physically inspect

○ Weigh & record data

HEALTH CHECKLIST

○ Active and alert

○ Eats regularly

○ Healthy shell

○ Clear, bright eyes

○ Healthy skin

○ Clear nose and vent

DIARY / NOTES:

DAILY ACTIVITY

Daily Activity	WEEK OF ___ DATE ___						
	SUN	MON	TUE	WED	THU	FRI	SAT
Feed Tortoise	○	○	○	○	○	○	○
Clean & refresh water bowl	○	○	○	○	○	○	○
Check temp / humidity	○	○	○	○	○	○	○
Clean waste Remove uneaten food	○	○	○	○	○	○	○
Visually inspect.	○	○	○	○	○	○	○
Use calcium supplements 1 x / 2-3 day	○	○	○	○	○	○	○
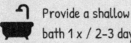 Provide a shallow bath 1 x / 2-3 day	○	○	○	○	○	○	○

NOTES:

WEEKLY ACTIVITY

📅 DATE: _____   📅 DATE: _____

WEEKLY ACTIVITY

- ○ Clean the habitat
- ○ Top up substrate
- ○ Clean any decorative rocks, plants etc
- ○ Physically inspect
- ○ Weigh & record data
- ○ _____

HEALTH CHECKLIST

- ○ Active and alert
- ○ Eats regularly
- ○ Healthy shell
- ○ Clear, bright eyes
- ○ Healthy skin
- ○ Clear nose and vent

DIARY / NOTES:

DAILY ACTIVITY

 Daily Activity

WEEK OF _____ DATE _____

	SUN	MON	TUE	WED	THU	FRI	SAT
Feed Tortoise	○	○	○	○	○	○	○
Clean & refresh water bowl	○	○	○	○	○	○	○
Check temp / humidity	○	○	○	○	○	○	○
Clean waste Remove uneaten food	○	○	○	○	○	○	○
Visually inspect.	○	○	○	○	○	○	○
20 Ca Use calcium supplements 1 x / 2-3 day	○	○	○	○	○	○	○
Provide a shallow bath 1 x / 2-3 day	○	○	○	○	○	○	○

NOTES:

WEEKLY ACTIVITY

📅 DATE: _____   📅 DATE: _____

WEEKLY ACTIVITY

○ Clean the habitat

○ Top up substrate

○ Clean any decorative rocks, plants etc

○ Physically inspect

○ Weigh & record data

○ _____

HEALTH CHECKLIST

○ Active and alert

○ Eats regularly

○ Healthy shell

○ Clear, bright eyes

○ Healthy skin

○ Clear nose and vent

DIARY / NOTES:

DAILY ACTIVITY

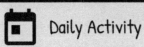 Daily Activity

WEEK OF _____ DATE _____

SUN MON TUE WED THU FRI SAT

 Feed Tortoise ○ ○ ○ ○ ○ ○ ○

 Clean & refresh water bowl ○ ○ ○ ○ ○ ○ ○

 Check temp / humidity ○ ○ ○ ○ ○ ○ ○

 Clean waste Remove uneaten food ○ ○ ○ ○ ○ ○ ○

 Visually inspect. ○ ○ ○ ○ ○ ○ ○

 Use calcium supplements 1 x / 2-3 day ○ ○ ○ ○ ○ ○ ○

 Provide a shallow bath 1 x / 2-3 day ○ ○ ○ ○ ○ ○ ○

NOTES:

WEEKLY ACTIVITY

📅 DATE: _____　　📅 DATE: _____

WEEKLY ACTIVITY

- ○ Clean the habitat
- ○ Top up substrate
- ○ Clean any decorative rocks, plants etc
- ○ Physically inspect
- ○ Weigh & record data
  _____

HEALTH CHECKLIST

- ○ Active and alert
- ○ Eats regularly
- ○ Healthy shell
- ○ Clear, bright eyes
- ○ Healthy skin
- ○ Clear nose and vent

DIARY / NOTES:

DAILY ACTIVITY

 Daily Activity

WEEK OF _____ DATE _____

	SUN	MON	TUE	WED	THU	FRI	SAT
Feed Tortoise	○	○	○	○	○	○	○
Clean & refresh water bowl	○	○	○	○	○	○	○
Check temp / humidity	○	○	○	○	○	○	○
Clean waste Remove uneaten food	○	○	○	○	○	○	○
Visually inspect.	○	○	○	○	○	○	○
Use calcium supplements 1 x / 2-3 day	○	○	○	○	○	○	○
Provide a shallow bath 1 x / 2-3 day	○	○	○	○	○	○	○

NOTES:

WEEKLY ACTIVITY

📅 DATE: _____

📅 DATE: _____

WEEKLY ACTIVITY

- ◯ Clean the habitat
- ◯ Top up substrate
- ◯ Clean any decorative rocks, plants etc
- ◯ Physically inspect
- ◯ Weigh & record data
- ◯ _____

HEALTH CHECKLIST

- ◯ Active and alert
- ◯ Eats regularly
- ◯ Healthy shell
- ◯ Clear, bright eyes
- ◯ Healthy skin
- ◯ Clear nose and vent

DIARY / NOTES:

DAILY ACTIVITY

 Daily Activity

WEEK OF [ ] DATE [ ]

	SUN	MON	TUE	WED	THU	FRI	SAT
Feed Tortoise	○	○	○	○	○	○	○
Clean & refresh water bowl	○	○	○	○	○	○	○
Check temp / humidity	○	○	○	○	○	○	○
Clean waste Remove uneaten food	○	○	○	○	○	○	○
Visually inspect.	○	○	○	○	○	○	○
Use calcium supplements 1 x / 2-3 day	○	○	○	○	○	○	○
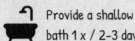 Provide a shallow bath 1 x / 2-3 day	○	○	○	○	○	○	○

NOTES:

WEEKLY ACTIVITY

📅 DATE: _____   📅 DATE: _____

WEEKLY ACTIVITY

- ⚪ Clean the habitat
- ⚪ Top up substrate
- ⚪ Clean any decorative rocks, plants etc
- ⚪ Physically inspect
- ⚪ Weigh & record data

HEALTH CHECKLIST

- ⚪ Active and alert
- ⚪ Eats regularly
- ⚪ Healthy shell
- ⚪ Clear, bright eyes
- ⚪ Healthy skin
- ⚪ Clear nose and vent

DIARY / NOTES:

DAILY ACTIVITY

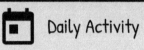 **Daily Activity**

WEEK OF ____ DATE ____

SUN	MON	TUE	WED	THU	FRI	SAT

 Feed Tortoise

○ ○ ○ ○ ○ ○ ○

 Clean & refresh water bowl

○ ○ ○ ○ ○ ○ ○

 Check temp / humidity

○ ○ ○ ○ ○ ○ ○

 Clean waste Remove uneaten food

○ ○ ○ ○ ○ ○ ○

 Visually inspect.

○ ○ ○ ○ ○ ○ ○

 Use calcium supplements 1 x / 2-3 day

○ ○ ○ ○ ○ ○ ○

 Provide a shallow bath 1 x / 2-3 day

○ ○ ○ ○ ○ ○ ○

NOTES:

WEEKLY ACTIVITY

📅 DATE: _____   📅 DATE: _____

WEEKLY ACTIVITY

- ○ Clean the habitat
- ○ Top up substrate
- ○ Clean any decorative rocks, plants etc
- ○ Physically inspect
- ○ Weigh & record data
- ○ _____

HEALTH CHECKLIST

- ○ Active and alert
- ○ Eats regularly
- ○ Healthy shell
- ○ Clear, bright eyes
- ○ Healthy skin
- ○ Clear nose and vent

DIARY / NOTES:

DAILY ACTIVITY

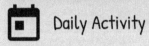 Daily Activity	WEEK OF _____ DATE _____						
	SUN	MON	TUE	WED	THU	FRI	SAT
Feed Tortoise	○	○	○	○	○	○	○
Clean & refresh water bowl	○	○	○	○	○	○	○
Check temp / humidity	○	○	○	○	○	○	○
Clean waste Remove uneaten food	○	○	○	○	○	○	○
Visually inspect.	○	○	○	○	○	○	○
Use calcium supplements 1 x / 2-3 day	○	○	○	○	○	○	○
Provide a shallow bath 1 x / 2-3 day	○	○	○	○	○	○	○

NOTES:

WEEKLY ACTIVITY

📅 DATE: _____   📅 DATE: _____

WEEKLY ACTIVITY

- ⚪ Clean the habitat
- ⚪ Top up substrate
- ⚪ Clean any decorative rocks, plants etc
- ⚪ Physically inspect
- ⚪ Weigh & record data
  _____

HEALTH CHECKLIST

- ⚪ Active and alert
- ⚪ Eats regularly
- ⚪ Healthy shell
- ⚪ Clear, bright eyes
- ⚪ Healthy skin
- ⚪ Clear nose and vent

DIARY / NOTES:

DAILY ACTIVITY

Daily Activity	WEEK OF ___ DATE ___						
	SUN	MON	TUE	WED	THU	FRI	SAT
Feed Tortoise	○	○	○	○	○	○	○
Clean & refresh water bowl	○	○	○	○	○	○	○
Check temp / humidity	○	○	○	○	○	○	○
Clean waste Remove uneaten food	○	○	○	○	○	○	○
Visually inspect.	○	○	○	○	○	○	○
Use calcium supplements 1 x / 2-3 day	○	○	○	○	○	○	○
Provide a shallow bath 1 x / 2-3 day	○	○	○	○	○	○	○

NOTES:

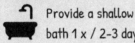

WEEKLY ACTIVITY

 DATE: _____

📅 DATE: _____

WEEKLY ACTIVITY

- ○ Clean the habitat
- ○ Top up substrate
- ○ Clean any decorative rocks, plants etc
- ○ Physically inspect
- ○ Weigh & record data
- _____

HEALTH CHECKLIST

- ○ Active and alert
- ○ Eats regularly
- ○ Healthy shell
- ○ Clear, bright eyes
- ○ Healthy skin
- ○ Clear nose and vent

DIARY / NOTES:

DAILY ACTIVITY

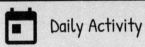 **Daily Activity**

WEEK OF _____ DATE _____

	SUN	MON	TUE	WED	THU	FRI	SAT
Feed Tortoise	○	○	○	○	○	○	○
Clean & refresh water bowl	○	○	○	○	○	○	○
Check temp / humidity	○	○	○	○	○	○	○
Clean waste Remove uneaten food	○	○	○	○	○	○	○
Visually inspect.	○	○	○	○	○	○	○
Use calcium supplements 1 x / 2-3 day	○	○	○	○	○	○	○
Provide a shallow bath 1 x / 2-3 day	○	○	○	○	○	○	○

NOTES:

WEEKLY ACTIVITY

📅 DATE: _____   📅 DATE: _____

WEEKLY ACTIVITY

- ⚪ Clean the habitat
- ⚪ Top up substrate
- ⚪ Clean any decorative rocks, plants etc
- ⚪ Physically inspect
- ⚪ Weigh & record data
- ⚪ _____

HEALTH CHECKLIST

- ⚪ Active and alert
- ⚪ Eats regularly
- ⚪ Healthy shell
- ⚪ Clear, bright eyes
- ⚪ Healthy skin
- ⚪ Clear nose and vent

DIARY / NOTES:

DAILY ACTIVITY

 Daily Activity

WEEK OF _____ DATE _____

	SUN	MON	TUE	WED	THU	FRI	SAT
Feed Tortoise	○	○	○	○	○	○	○
Clean & refresh water bowl	○	○	○	○	○	○	○
Check temp / humidity	○	○	○	○	○	○	○
Clean waste Remove uneaten food	○	○	○	○	○	○	○
Visually inspect.	○	○	○	○	○	○	○
Use calcium supplements 1 x / 2-3 day	○	○	○	○	○	○	○
Provide a shallow bath 1 x / 2-3 day	○	○	○	○	○	○	○

NOTES:

WEEKLY ACTIVITY

📅 DATE: _____   📅 DATE: _____

WEEKLY ACTIVITY

○ Clean the habitat

○ Top up substrate

○ Clean any decorative rocks, plants etc

○ Physically inspect

○ Weigh & record data

_____

HEALTH CHECKLIST

○ Active and alert

○ Eats regularly

○ Healthy shell

○ Clear, bright eyes

○ Healthy skin

○ Clear nose and vent

DIARY / NOTES:

DAILY ACTIVITY

 Daily Activity

WEEK OF _____ DATE _____

SUN	MON	TUE	WED	THU	FRI	SAT

 Feed Tortoise

| ○ | ○ | ○ | ○ | ○ | ○ | ○ |

 Clean & refresh water bowl

| ○ | ○ | ○ | ○ | ○ | ○ | ○ |

 Check temp / humidity

| ○ | ○ | ○ | ○ | ○ | ○ | ○ |

 Clean waste
Remove uneaten food

| ○ | ○ | ○ | ○ | ○ | ○ | ○ |

 Visually inspect.

| ○ | ○ | ○ | ○ | ○ | ○ | ○ |

 Use calcium supplements 1 x / 2-3 day

| ○ | ○ | ○ | ○ | ○ | ○ | ○ |

 Provide a shallow bath 1 x / 2-3 day

| ○ | ○ | ○ | ○ | ○ | ○ | ○ |

NOTES:

WEEKLY ACTIVITY

 DATE: _____   📅 DATE: _____

WEEKLY ACTIVITY

- ○ Clean the habitat
- ○ Top up substrate
- ○ Clean any decorative rocks, plants etc
- ○ Physically inspect
- ○ Weigh & record data

HEALTH CHECKLIST

- ○ Active and alert
- ○ Eats regularly
- ○ Healthy shell
- ○ Clear, bright eyes
- ○ Healthy skin
- ○ Clear nose and vent

DIARY / NOTES:

DAILY ACTIVITY

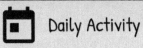 Daily Activity

	WEEK OF	DATE					
	SUN	MON	TUE	WED	THU	FRI	SAT

 Feed Tortoise ○ ○ ○ ○ ○ ○ ○

 Clean & refresh water bowl ○ ○ ○ ○ ○ ○ ○

 Check temp / humidity ○ ○ ○ ○ ○ ○ ○

 Clean waste Remove uneaten food ○ ○ ○ ○ ○ ○ ○

 Visually inspect. ○ ○ ○ ○ ○ ○ ○

 Use calcium supplements 1 x / 2-3 day ○ ○ ○ ○ ○ ○ ○

 Provide a shallow bath 1 x / 2-3 day ○ ○ ○ ○ ○ ○ ○

NOTES:

WEEKLY ACTIVITY

📅 DATE: _____   📅 DATE: _____

WEEKLY ACTIVITY

- ⚪ Clean the habitat
- ⚪ Top up substrate
- ⚪ Clean any decorative rocks, plants etc
- ⚪ Physically inspect
- ⚪ Weigh & record data
  - _____

HEALTH CHECKLIST

- ⚪ Active and alert
- ⚪ Eats regularly
- ⚪ Healthy shell
- ⚪ Clear, bright eyes
- ⚪ Healthy skin
- ⚪ Clear nose and vent

DIARY / NOTES:

DAILY ACTIVITY

 Daily Activity

WEEK OF _____ DATE _____

	SUN	MON	TUE	WED	THU	FRI	SAT
Feed Tortoise	○	○	○	○	○	○	○
Clean & refresh water bowl	○	○	○	○	○	○	○
Check temp / humidity	○	○	○	○	○	○	○
Clean waste Remove uneaten food	○	○	○	○	○	○	○
Visually inspect.	○	○	○	○	○	○	○
Use calcium supplements 1 x / 2-3 day	○	○	○	○	○	○	○
Provide a shallow bath 1 x / 2-3 day	○	○	○	○	○	○	○

NOTES:

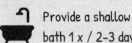

WEEKLY ACTIVITY

📅 DATE: _____   📅 DATE: _____

WEEKLY ACTIVITY

○ Clean the habitat

○ Top up substrate

○ Clean any decorative rocks, plants etc

○ Physically inspect

○ Weigh & record data

○ _____

HEALTH CHECKLIST

○ Active and alert

○ Eats regularly

○ Healthy shell

○ Clear, bright eyes

○ Healthy skin

○ Clear nose and vent

DIARY / NOTES:

DAILY ACTIVITY

 Daily Activity

WEEK OF [   ] DATE [   ]

	SUN	MON	TUE	WED	THU	FRI	SAT
Feed Tortoise	○	○	○	○	○	○	○
Clean & refresh water bowl	○	○	○	○	○	○	○
Check temp / humidity	○	○	○	○	○	○	○
Clean waste Remove uneaten food	○	○	○	○	○	○	○
Visually inspect.	○	○	○	○	○	○	○
Use calcium supplements 1 x / 2-3 day	○	○	○	○	○	○	○
Provide a shallow bath 1 x / 2-3 day	○	○	○	○	○	○	○

NOTES:

WEEKLY ACTIVITY

📅 DATE: _____   📅 DATE: _____

WEEKLY ACTIVITY

- ○ Clean the habitat
- ○ Top up substrate
- ○ Clean any decorative rocks, plants etc
- ○ Physically inspect
- ○ Weigh & record data
- ○

HEALTH CHECKLIST

- ○ Active and alert
- ○ Eats regularly
- ○ Healthy shell
- ○ Clear, bright eyes
- ○ Healthy skin
- ○ Clear nose and vent

DIARY / NOTES:

DAILY ACTIVITY

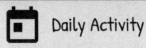 Daily Activity	WEEK OF ____ DATE _____						
	SUN	MON	TUE	WED	THU	FRI	SAT
Feed Tortoise	○	○	○	○	○	○	○
Clean & refresh water bowl	○	○	○	○	○	○	○
Check temp / humidity	○	○	○	○	○	○	○
Clean waste Remove uneaten food	○	○	○	○	○	○	○
Visually inspect.	○	○	○	○	○	○	○
Use calcium supplements 1 x / 2-3 day	○	○	○	○	○	○	○
Provide a shallow bath 1 x / 2-3 day	○	○	○	○	○	○	○

NOTES:

WEEKLY ACTIVITY

📅 DATE: _____   📅 DATE: _____

WEEKLY ACTIVITY

- ○ Clean the habitat
- ○ Top up substrate
- ○ Clean any decorative rocks, plants etc
- ○ Physically inspect
- ○ Weigh & record data
  - _____

HEALTH CHECKLIST

- ○ Active and alert
- ○ Eats regularly
- ○ Healthy shell
- ○ Clear, bright eyes
- ○ Healthy skin
- ○ Clear nose and vent

DIARY / NOTES:

DAILY ACTIVITY

 Daily Activity

WEEK OF _____ DATE _____

	SUN	MON	TUE	WED	THU	FRI	SAT
Feed Tortoise	○	○	○	○	○	○	○
Clean & refresh water bowl	○	○	○	○	○	○	○
Check temp / humidity	○	○	○	○	○	○	○
Clean waste Remove uneaten food	○	○	○	○	○	○	○
Visually inspect.	○	○	○	○	○	○	○
Use calcium supplements 1 x / 2-3 day	○	○	○	○	○	○	○
Provide a shallow bath 1 x / 2-3 day	○	○	○	○	○	○	○

NOTES:

WEEKLY ACTIVITY

📅 DATE: _____   📅 DATE: _____

WEEKLY ACTIVITY	HEALTH CHECKLIST

WEEKLY ACTIVITY

○ Clean the habitat

○ Top up substrate

○ Clean any decorative rocks, plants etc

○ Physically inspect

○ Weigh & record data

○ _____

HEALTH CHECKLIST

○ Active and alert

○ Eats regularly

○ Healthy shell

○ Clear, bright eyes

○ Healthy skin

○ Clear nose and vent

DIARY / NOTES:

DAILY ACTIVITY

Daily Activity	WEEK OF ___ DATE ___
	SUN MON TUE WED THU FRI SAT

		SUN	MON	TUE	WED	THU	FRI	SAT
	Feed Tortoise	◯	◯	◯	◯	◯	◯	◯
	Clean & refresh water bowl	◯	◯	◯	◯	◯	◯	◯
	Check temp / humidity	◯	◯	◯	◯	◯	◯	◯
	Clean waste Remove uneaten food	◯	◯	◯	◯	◯	◯	◯
	Visually inspect.	◯	◯	◯	◯	◯	◯	◯
	Use calcium supplements 1 x / 2-3 day	◯	◯	◯	◯	◯	◯	◯
	Provide a shallow bath 1 x / 2-3 day	◯	◯	◯	◯	◯	◯	◯

NOTES:

WEEKLY ACTIVITY

📅 DATE: _____   📅 DATE: _____

WEEKLY ACTIVITY

○ Clean the habitat

○ Top up substrate

○ Clean any decorative rocks, plants etc

○ Physically inspect

○ Weigh & record data

HEALTH CHECKLIST

○ Active and alert

○ Eats regularly

○ Healthy shell

○ Clear, bright eyes

○ Healthy skin

○ Clear nose and vent

DIARY / NOTES:

DAILY ACTIVITY

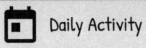 **Daily Activity**

WEEK OF _____ DATE _____

SUN MON TUE WED THU FRI SAT

 Feed Tortoise

○ ○ ○ ○ ○ ○ ○

 Clean & refresh water bowl

○ ○ ○ ○ ○ ○ ○

 Check temp / humidity

○ ○ ○ ○ ○ ○ ○

 Clean waste Remove uneaten food

○ ○ ○ ○ ○ ○ ○

 Visually inspect.

○ ○ ○ ○ ○ ○ ○

 Use calcium supplements 1 x / 2-3 day

○ ○ ○ ○ ○ ○ ○

 Provide a shallow bath 1 x / 2-3 day

○ ○ ○ ○ ○ ○ ○

NOTES:

WEEKLY ACTIVITY

📅 DATE: [   ]   📅 DATE: [   ]

WEEKLY ACTIVITY

- ◯ Clean the habitat
- ◯ Top up substrate
- ◯ Clean any decorative rocks, plants etc
- ◯ Physically inspect
- ◯ Weigh & record data
- ◯ [   ]

HEALTH CHECKLIST

- ◯ Active and alert
- ◯ Eats regularly
- ◯ Healthy shell
- ◯ Clear, bright eyes
- ◯ Healthy skin
- ◯ Clear nose and vent

DIARY / NOTES:

DAILY ACTIVITY

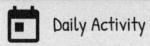 **Daily Activity**

WEEK OF ___ DATE ___

SUN MON TUE WED THU FRI SAT

 Feed Tortoise
○ ○ ○ ○ ○ ○ ○

 Clean & refresh water bowl
○ ○ ○ ○ ○ ○ ○

 Check temp / humidity
○ ○ ○ ○ ○ ○ ○

 Clean waste Remove uneaten food
○ ○ ○ ○ ○ ○ ○

 Visually inspect.
○ ○ ○ ○ ○ ○ ○

 Use calcium supplements 1 x / 2-3 day
○ ○ ○ ○ ○ ○ ○

 Provide a shallow bath 1 x / 2-3 day
○ ○ ○ ○ ○ ○ ○

NOTES:

WEEKLY ACTIVITY

📅 DATE: _____   📅 DATE: _____

WEEKLY ACTIVITY

- ○ Clean the habitat
- ○ Top up substrate
- ○ Clean any decorative rocks, plants etc
- ○ Physically inspect
- ○ Weigh & record data
- ○ _____

HEALTH CHECKLIST

- ○ Active and alert
- ○ Eats regularly
- ○ Healthy shell
- ○ Clear, bright eyes
- ○ Healthy skin
- ○ Clear nose and vent

DIARY / NOTES:

NOTES:

MY PET
TORTOISE LOGBOOK